Acknowledgments

Thanks to the editors of *The Rialto, Ambit, Smiths Knoll, Envoi,* and *Iota* in whose publications versions of some of the poems in this collection have appeared. Thanks to Patricia Oxley of *Acumen,* whose invitation to read at the celebration of The English Riviera's new Geopark status in 2008 was the impetus for 'Breaking Point' and 'End of Term'. 'Safe' was a prize winner in the 2006 Challenging Poverty Poetry Competition.

'Creek', 'End of Term', 'Mute', 'Inside', and 'Linden Tree', appeared in *The Visitors* (Cinnamon, 2010); 'Ghost Moon, 'Morning' and 'Test' appeared in *The Ground Beneath Her Feet* (Cinnamon, 2008).

Special thanks to Bill Greenwell and Greta Stoddart for their inspiring teaching and encouragement; to Pascale Petit for her workshop on Animals and Myth; to the Mincing Poets and to Diana Gittins for rigorous critique; to Elly Nobbs for being my first 'perfect' reader; to my many poet friends from Devon and around the world for their encouragement and support; and to my editor, Jan Fortune-Wood. Special thanks also to my parents for starting me on the road to poetry via A.A. Milne, Lewis Carroll and Hilaire Belloc. But most of all, thanks to David, Sophie, Natasha and Richard Douglas, for everything.

Contents

Linden Tree

Candling the Eggs

SALLY DOUGLAS

Published by Cinnamon Press
Meirion House
Glan yr afon
Tanygrisiau
Blaenau Ffestiniog
Gwynedd
LL41 3SU
www.cinnamonpress.com

ISBN: 978-1-907090-26-4
British Library Cataloguing in Publication Data. A CIP record for this book can be obtained from the British Library.

Designed and typeset in Palatino by Cinnamon Press. Cover design by Cottia Fortune-Wood from original artwork 'House' by Aleksandr Tkachuk, agency © Dreamstime.com. Printed in Poland
Cinnamon Press is represented in the UK by Inpress Ltd www.inpressbooks.co.uk and in Wales by the Welsh Books Council www.cllc.org.uk.

Winter Children

Candling the Eggs

Linden Tree

Mute

If you had done what you say you have done
you would have scars.

If this had happened as you say,
someone would have noticed.

If he had done this thing you say he has done,
you would have spoken then.

If what you say is true, there would be records,
not poems.

We have looked for records.
There are none.

If what you say is true, the dark would be spooling out
behind you.

But all you have done is create these things,
opaque as swans.

Inside

The breath of a wall
nothing but a shimmer of air on a hot road
nothing but a curtain of change between inside and out

Nothing but lips pressed together
not taped
not sewn but pressed
like hands in prayer

A hand against nothing can make a wall

You slide your fingertips over the cold nothing
open your mouth
the words come out
          frantic as birds against glass

Path

There is a silent line
under her skin.
Trace its route from earlobe, neck,
down to the margin of breast,
skimming the border between front and back
where she is always cold.

Sweeping, silver, to the groin,
and down like a pungent trickle
that dried many years ago,
then kissing the braided cavity of knee
and the ankle's egg-like bone.

It's all that's left from when
he stitched her with harebells
culled from the verges
of the Wissenweg –
the thread so fine
it hardly hurt at all.

Linden Tree

Thence up he flew, and on the Tree of Life…
Sat like a Cormorant

Paradise Lost: Milton

Afterwards, she remembers feathers.
Feathers caped around her,
wings straitjacketing her arms
as if she might have struggled.

How she thought an angel was behind her
until that terrible pressure:
the black mask snaking over her shoulder
the flicker at her breast.

Oh, but the words
sliding over her – words dark as olives,
the unhearable words –
words slick as oil.

Afterwards she wants to clothe herself in feathers
feel the barbs, the pinions,
but all she has is leaves.

Outside the Wall

He leans back against its curve:
stones press his skin air-thin against his bones.
Scapulae, vertebrae, ribs.

Each stone is a word he wants to swallow:
if he scrapes away the mortar, takes, eats,
he could make a hole the size of himself.
He looks around for a tool: a stick, a bone.

But the woman sits on the riverbank
holding one hand up to the sun
so she can see the blood glowing.

He pushes back, harder.
If he pushes hard enough the stones will enter him that way.
Granite, slate, flint.

Silence

The silences are what she likes best.
They slide between them like grey rivers
like long tongues searching for sweetness.

She pulls honeysuckle flowers off the stem,
sucks the whisper from their throats
catches it with her tongue.

Abdication

Adam's task was the invention of language, to name each thing.

Because they do not dazzle her,
she gets to name the white things.
Teeth, feathers, bandages, the old man's beard, bones.
Plaster casts, the face in the river, the sand.

She can feel their shapes with her tongue.
Ointment, ghosts, marble, snow, paper, kaolin, milk.
Tissues, tampons, sanitary towels, lies,
the small round pills, the sheets, the suds.

Matryoshka

She carves her daughter out of linden:
truth-wood. A baby smaller
than the smallest humming-bird.

Paints white gouache swaddling,
black-ink eyes. The tip
of the finest feather is her brush.

Next, to keep the baby safe, she makes
herself. And then another self, to nest
that one within.

Carves many selves, each bigger, thicker,
harder: swollen skittles, arms varnished
to their sides.

If one goes missing
no one will ever know.

Golem

First he took *I am here*:
screwed it up and put it in his pocket,
worked it into clothy shreds.

I am good he folded neatly, flat;
laid it on his tongue.
Took the proffered wine to help it down.

Then bigger things.
I am free.
The wall is for our own good.
He found that if he closed his eyes it helped.

We deserved it.

And when the soldiers came
he swallowed everything
not gagging even once.

Star

A cold star
hooked in her throat.
Years of silence.
But one day it will blacken,
become pure gravity –
and then she'll hear her bones,
talking.

The Robe

She threads her warp on a strange loom;
weaves red symbols through the white.

Ovid: Metamorphoses

You swaddled me with furious proofs,
wrapped me in cloths bleached bright by rage.
And as I grew, I joined you at the loom:
wove shadows of the things I'd never seen.

Now I prowl the riverbank,
dragging the robe like broken wings.
I can't unpick this history you've stitched to me.

Origami

She writes words on white paper
folds them into swans
to send down the river.

She thinks swans are better than bottles
because her words will not be tainted
by the memory of milk or wine or beer or pills

and swans cannot be smashed into weapons
in the Saturday dark.

She's made a flock of speckled swans.

But the one she sets down on the river's puckered skin
is white.

Letter

The house martins have finally come back.
I watch them from my window. Father hates
the mess, but he can't manage ladders any more.

I'm fine. You needn't worry.
I think of you, though I don't always write.
It's not so bad here. Peaceful now the troops have gone.

Father's thin as twigs. Each day I find it harder
to unfold him from the night. I think of paper dolls
down in the cellar. Your suitcase with the broken lock.

The blossom from the cherry is like paper on the ground.
I remember you, in the attic,
cutting paper into tiny tiny squares.

I hope this finds you.

The Snake Claims Kinship to the Swan

We were brothers.
See, that neck echoes mine.
We're crucks split
from the one curved tree.
Threaten us: we hiss.

We were sisters:
close as a clutch in our reedy nest.
Cold nights we twined
like plaited bay;
summer days we arced
the symmetry of heart
and caught the sky.

Won't anyone believe?

I was the fall-guy.
That angel man, he took my feathers, body, legs.
Split my tongue.

Candling the Eggs

Carefully as a jeweller – fore-finger to apex,
thumb to base – she holds each one close
to the forty watt bulb set up in the corner of the barn.

Leans forward, as if to an airless bell-jar
in an eighteenth century study, assaying
futures as the egg inhales light.

There are three possible conclusions:
fertilised, edible, bad.

She thinks of how these dark trawls
are cloaked in words of light.

Last night, for instance, lamping in the fields –
rabbits, frozen in the rapture of the beam;
the shotgun's long pragmatic aim.

Tomorrow, it won't be light that candles
her, but slender waves of sound.

Carefully she holds each one, as if it were
a tiny skull: thumb to occipital crest,
fore-finger to unclosing fontanelle.

Aubade

the slow slide of rain
the slow turn of a page

a book with the pages lost
a book with the pages never printed

the long grey sky
the vacant night

pillows, the soft
soft pillows pressing down

the slow stretch to morning
the clamour of dawn

the tattered light
the crows

Premature

for Oliver

Time lies like stones under water
heavy pebbles
anchoring the days.

You lie on a rind of light
sleep and breathe on the curves of moon and arm,
in moments pared from silver coins.

Unclinging, you curl
into spaces broken from the air
and open your eyes –

your eyes the colour of slate
but clear as water
moving over heavy stones.

Ghost Moon

That ghost moon follows me all day.

Like letters to dead people,
sliding through my letterbox,
years after the funeral.

It's a faded transfer on the sky,
a retinal scar.

I write – the shadow of my head across the page,
the sun's hot hand pressing down on my neck.

Going Back

It ends like this:

I'm crouching, hugging my knees –
scuffed Clarks sandals, well-picked scab –
leaning into the shallow valley
with the familiar street
neat as a model village.
The light's like water, fills it to the brim.
Licks my toes. Butterfly fish
swim in through open doorways,
out of windows.

She can't see me watching her
as she shakes a mat, calls the dog,
turns to go inside.

I want to kick my feet bare,
dive down the hill.

But I'd drown in that golden air.

Creek

A low moon through the trees
and the tide's pulse inwards –
nets, rods, lines stowed neatly,
and a dark wake following.

Bumping the sludgy edge, the boat
shivers, lets the tide slide around it.
Empty branches fracture the sky.

And I think of those springs when
need was so strong that the road became river;
that pull of things, over and back,
like your slow breath sliding;
and the fish, gulping.

The moon is smeared over the river's skin,
like unction. I turn with the tide.

Source Code

i
Sun-sapped,
pulled by the moon:
I make the cracked bed sing.

ii
A spring, a double twist,
a muddy pool,
a splice, the binary of light and dark.

iii
I breach, retreat, and breach again,
but each time now I'm
flung far past the pivot.

iv
I rage, I sleep, I rage again.
My oxbow claws
cling to a failing crux.

v
In the hard wood, the heartwood,
an echo of my voice,
the beetle's knock, which no one will decrypt.
But feel the heartbeat, ticking
in parched hollows.

vi
The model grows to be
the thing itself. Cannot compute
the balance.

Breaking

You don't notice it at first,
the wind's drag on the surface –
like words that go unheard
because you're thinking
of something else.

You don't feel it as it frets and pulls,
as it sets up
circling shivers
under the water's skin –

but behind you
there are whispers
and leeward eddies steepen the swell.

It's later,
much later,
that the wave hits the shore.

Tripped by the sudden, startling land,
everything collapses into turbulence and swirl –
swash, backwash –
flinging the shingle past the break-
point bar
dragging back the finer grit,
the shells

the strafing sand.

End of Term

'...Exeter St David's, Dawlish, Teignmouth, Newton Abbot...'

The train has always slowed here, at the edge.
Back then I'd be hoping for the water's fling and scour
against my twin-ghost image in the glass:
a baptism I didn't need to feel.

But now I watch the inland side,
where daily frictions strip
the past wide open.
I trace the hard-ribbed lines of sediment
to find the restless sand.

Where two things meet is where you feel things most.

Tonight I'll wade into the ocean.
The surface will be a bright cold wire
rising round me, upwards, up towards to my throat,
slicing through my body like a scan.

Thumbelina

Last night I had a
baby. She was tiny —
even smaller than my
thumb.
Her heartbeat fluttered
mothlike in my palm.

The cot was vast. Instead
I laid her in a matchbox,
nested her in scraps of silk,
and scattered unstrung pearls
for her to play. I slid the
cover closed so she'd be safe.

Then I forgot I'd had a
baby. Life went by. Emptying
my locker, wondering
why am I at school? my
fingers found an unfamiliar
box, light as the moon.

Inside: my baby, dried
out like a leaf, her hollow
cheeks transparent, and
her tiny hands like claws;
a paper husk now sighing
into dust.

In morning's pallid light I
heave myself from my
uneasy bed. Inside me you
remind me you're still
there.
            I don't think I
can do this.

Grounded

There's been a vagueness in the corner
for some time now

Something crouches:
wings laced with threadbare light
infibulations of mornings that haven't yet dawned

When it stirs
dust puffs from it in small eddies
like manifested sweat
or broken moth

Yesterday I realised
what it was, this
small revolutionary

Today I have brought it flies and mice
because its eyes are like empty owls
and I want to fill them with flight

but still it sits,
listless as winter grass.

Hoof

Przewalski's Horse

I wanted to follow the paths of the Yellow Horse.
For he was born in the night
and in the morning was ready to run.
For with his father's teeth at his tail
he could run forever.
So I placed a single fingertip
in the well-trodden furrows
that led from feeding ground to sleep,
and the bone grew wide and round.

I wanted to follow the paths of the Yellow Horse.
For his shadows are on the cave wall.
For he can hear the quiet stars.
So with my hard wide fingertip
I dug through ancient laminations of snow.

I wanted to follow the Yellow Horse.
With all that was left – my single fingertip –
I traced the map of his tracks.
But could not feel.

Wayland the Poet

for Bill Greenwell

His hands are tattooed black
with coaldust; firescale's
welded to his skin.

But iron's like a dream to him:
words are more substantial now.
He brings them up to forging heat,
hammers value into them,
drawing and fullering,
punching and drifting alien chunks
into the heart of the old;
wedges them together so tight
they're grafted into something new.
His burnished words
bind clouds and fire and thunder to the page.

His pockets are full of charred pencils.

Shore Leave

i.m. Stanley Godwin Scarth Rowe, d.24.5.1941 on HMS Hood, aged seventeen

He sets the kettle on the range
and as it starts to tick
flicks non-existent dust
from dauntless epaulettes.

His brothers in their rolled-up sleeves
and flannel shorts worn thin as winter light
sit cross-legged, waiting.

His mother at the window
watches the slow plunge
into evening, draws the blackout blind.

The tea in the cup is the bronze of the sky.
In the harbour the sea is wine-dark.

Morning

Daylight – anatomical,
precise – slides between us,
fillets us apart.

In those last seconds,
still fused to you by the heat of sleep's oven,
I listen to the birds –
            already prised from night –

and wait for the flaking,
the stripping down to bones.

The Shape of Faith

Driving home, with autumn stretching light
so gold and thin, I brake to let a cat
shear past my wheels, leap through the hedge.

I stall the car.

Today I watched you watch your children play,
and listened to the scaling of your lungs –
counted off each breath, one less, one less.

Today, like every day, you wrapped yourself
in shining convolutions: made Mobius strips to prove
inside is out, and power is kind. But

when you shape your faith to me words
slide, and will not stay attached to proper things.

Good

Merciful

Love –

each one traces coils of martyrs'guts spilled
dark on soil, climbs Escher's cold recursive stairs.

Yellow leaves skate on the air's planes,
lilt to the ground, tracing lines
of pressure and resistance as they fall.

At the hedge foot, shaggy inkcaps
turn to slime. Beyond the hedge
the stubbled field is empty to the sky.

Winter Children

Collateral Damage

Genesis, 22. 1-14

A mountain in Moriah, he said. God wills,
and off we trot, as innocent as sleep. We leave
before the sun, with the ass carrying the fire.

We come back silent as hills.

Now I dream of rams pierced with bright thorns,
and drowse restlessly among the flock. I look to the clear
sky and see smoke. I burn in the night,
and cannot speak.

I watch the old man, who has made many altars.

I wrap myself in fleece,
and stroke a bevelled blade.

Winter Children

The winter children
wheel and arc
above the stuttering hinterlands of the city
their faces flattened by the air.

The winter children have faces of damp clay
mean as pinch-pots
features unformed as creeping dunes.

Their words are unfixed guttering.
Their cry like herring gulls on yawling winds,
like fingernails on glass.

What are these winter children
whose skin is damp tissue,
whose eyes are thumbprints,
whose hands are brittle with lime,
fingers red and scaled like feral pigeons' feet;
whose abstract nouns have been taken out like teeth?

Prised from a pomegranate husk
in the inverted dark
the children of winter now razor the skies
like angels without souls:

clay doves
shedding pieces of themselves upon the rubble,
never closing splintered eyes
even when the dust falls thick as ash.

Safe

i
A red playhouse with
fabric walls
which arc in the wind.

ii
Under her pillow,
a toy gun and a snake
just in case.

iii
Tiny Tears always lost
her legs and arms somehow,
and later, her head.

iv
Dads are just for
Christmas, as transient
as moles.

v
A few cuts
here
and there.

vi
Under the pillow
a mobile phone, her pills
to keep her safe.

vii
Can't take the
baby
to college.

Raw Material

Someone found it in the gutter
nudged between kerb and camber
early one morning
after yesterday had been sluiced clean

And someone found it in the muck that spurted up
when they stood on the edge
of a paving slab
on the High Street

and stuck to the underside
of a café table
a pearl grey globule
brittled by air

Someone found it in the late night bus shelter
after the last bus had gone
and in the tiny skull of the mouse that got cooked
inside a malt and raisin loaf

and in the dirty rainbow behind Clapham Junction
on a Monday lunchtime in November
and in a left-over slice of pizza
and

And when they had these bits of it
the people didn't know
what use they were
but couldn't bear to let them go

so they stuffed them in drawers
with orphaned keys and batteries and old films that hadn't
been developed
and never would be now

Then something took the little bits of it
that lay bewildered at the backs of drawers
and made a fifteen minute golden girl

to be burnt in fire
ground to powder
scattered to the air

Role Play: Therapy in Three Parts

Patient

When you've left home,
they said.
So he left home.

When you've got children of your own,
they said.
So he built a house on salt-drenched sand.

When they're both dead,
they said.

So he waited till they died.
But it all still flickers like a broken film
strobing at the corner of his eye.

Actor

He starts like this:
Leichner 5 and *9,* slick as butter,
skating the planes of his face.
28 for the shadows.
Black around the eyes.
The flick of a match:
lit, spent.

Then, to brighten himself
in that bleached bowl of light:
he takes a cocktail stick
to gouge out carmine, white;
stabs careful dots
tight in the eye's soft angles.

Fossil Hunter

He stumps over the shale beds
which slump from the undercliff,
that brink where land falters,
loses balance.

.

He picks over spoils
like a crow at road-kill.
Places the shapes of the dead
in a red plastic bucket.

When he gets home he'll grind them to powder
trying to find their hearts.

Test

Shadows
are always there,
but you don't see them
if the light's not on.
True or False?

Edward thinks it's true.

All day at school, words
hiss behind shadows, are whispers
that he can't quite get.
Strip-lights flicker,
sickly in the sun; hum
to themselves above him.
The window's a bright square.

On the page, letters
rearrange themselves.

You can see because light comes
from your eyes.
True or False?

Edward closes his eyes.

Opaque means
something lets light through,
like a window. True or False?

Eyes closed, Edward can still see the window's ghost.
Eyes open, and it's a black shadow
floating on the surface of the page,
disturbing words. They twist and squirm
like tadpoles.

Apotheosis

i. How will you hold me,
me who barely knows of 'hold',
but feels the roots of smiles?

You will be a baby in a matchbox,
no bigger than my thumb.

ii. How will you buckle down the scrawl of me,
dot and line and inkblot?

I'll sculpt you like a grain of rice.
Bind and swaddle. Swaddle and bind.

iii. How will I grow old,
not even yet grown young?

I'll shape you
out of gingerbread: bake
your tender bones.
You won't run out with foxes.

iv. Will you always smile?

My smiles and yours are rooted deep.
The woodsman cannot cut out your white heart,
and mirrors tell a kind of truth.

v. Will you stay?

I'll pillow my head with yours,
and take you where I go. Forever
breathe you in. Never exhale.
My angel, my archangel:
my power, throne, dominion.

The Thoughts of Things: Scissors Dream

Everything desires to move towards its final purpose

Aristotle

I lie here, hug my edges
in the dark –

dream of
greaseproof paper rustling
as it's divided from itself

taut string
releasing

stiff card moaning

the tremor of a severed hair

And once — and oh I dream and dream of this
a chicken's skin:
its breast caressed me as I sheared
that cold elastic sheath
and liberated bone
I brood on this
I brood and dream

And now – her hands on silver-spidered arms
open the drawer
stroke me tenderly

I am knife doubled
I am knife to the power of myself

I could slash her pain away

tip edge
coming together
my blades shine
with the blooming

Do not close the drawer
Love me
I will open up for you

Transmissions

Search for dead babies
in disused cemeteries
The buzzing in the trees
is not the bees.

Give them food and cannabis
so they sleep.
The drumming in the trees
is not the bees.

Salvage the whale
that's washed up on the beach.
Stop your ears against the buzzing:
it is nothing like the bees.

The trains have stopped. There
are no volunteers.
The water bleeds
like autumn from the trees.

Don't let people
watch the water flooding in.
Listen for the thrumming
from the trees.

Grind the whale to bone meal.
Use as fuel.
Listen to the grey wind
in the trees.

There's a new smell
of stale camp-fire on the wind.
That humming in the air is
not the bees.

Caught

Call me Ishmael, he said.

The names had never mattered.
It was the immediacy of it all,
creeping through the mouseness of night.
Hours to go till light would strain
the seams of other people's sleep.

The heels were high, and clacked like tongues.
So I swung them from my fingers
and the pavement
cut my feet.

But down at the seafront, where
blank kiosks slept,
and the flat sands glimmered just beyond eyes,
I dropped the shoes
and let him lick the salt from my skin.

Why I have the Embalmed Body of a Tramp on my Roof Garden

He was the one who would never
come inside: knew the duplicity
of walls. Roofs pressed so hard on him.

They'd got him once, long ago,
after the forest had arched its hands in bogus blessing,
meshed its fingers to a tight-laced
sweet-faced cage.

He wouldn't be conned again. No more
trails of promises, gleaming like milk teeth
dropped from the rotting mouth of a fairy's sack.
No more gingerbread.

Always the flicker in his eye –
the pressing earth,
        the clanging furnace door –
the gnawed and scattered bones.

My gift to him. The open sky, a canvas sheet against the rain.
    A husk of future,
safer than the past.

The Stalker

I'm practising:
hiding in the gaps and folds of things.
Places you don't know you've left a space.
The cracked spines of old paperbacks.
The belly of a hole punch.
A grater's razor-smiles.

I'm getting good.
I've come a long long way from dust in air, mould
in forgotten coffee cups, grime
in the sweaty crevices of you.
Now I'm liquid; slight as sunshine
jumping from a blade.

I spy from the eyes of vanished children,
flickering pixels, shackled margins.
Twist myself into your keyboard, feel
you through the vowels, the S, the T –
your thumb firm on the spacebar, your
smallest finger gentle on the *Enter*, the *Return*.

I'll do it soon. I'm nearly there.
I'll slowly, slowly, peel the edge of you.
A tiny flap is all I need: a shaving nick,
a lip cracked with the winter cold.
I'll open you and slide myself
right under the meniscus of your skin.

Dolls

We saw the pictures on the news
the children with their bellies swollen
as if another child was hidden inside

You'd told me they were starving

But my friend Judy's mum
told her
they ate too much

Judy's mum
her eyes sliding away from yours
those children shrinking to a small white dot

Judy far away from me
on the carpet with her dolls

The Undoing

After I had woken night
I realised I had made a mistake.
The further north I travelled,
the louder were its voices in my head,
and the more the shadows marched
in long files like black feathers.

So I built a city
where light gagged the voices of night
and the owls were blind.

Now I wait in the dry pools of streetlamps,
search the nine million names of lullaby
for the one I need.

Visit

He has no idea why he is in this room,
how many stairs he has climbed, why
he is looking from this tall window down
into that empty street.

He has no idea who these people are: this bearded man
with plangent face, this woman with silent hands.
Why his father brought him here. Why they are sad.

In his pocket, a black twist of shrapnel,
a trophy from the street. He slips it
onto their mantelpiece: a gift.

Years later he remembers them
as kind, old, Jewish.

What's Left to Do

The dog snuffing puffballs, me breathing
autumn. The woods so still – far gunshots held
by the air, the mist like cotton wadding
in the day's flak-jacket.

When the dog yipped, I thought of the old times:
truffle shaved over a poached duck-egg, good wine.
I didn't expect to find the world's womb,
shrunk small, nested in a fallen tree.
A misshapen bladder: torn, stitched, torn.
          The dog quivered, backed away.

I picked it up. It was hollow as a skull.

Half way down the hill, where the ground
recedes like diseased gums, and tree-roots make
damp caves of leaf-mould, I scraped out a grave.

Pastoral

After the car had left
she walked out of the door
without locking it
without even listening for the quiet snick
walked down through the dark blue pastures
where the cow used to graze
before the bonfires
down past the barn where
she had collected owl feathers
for the striped jug on the dresser
down to the stream
no longer white with china clay.

To the Artist

Do not give me feathers.
Give me scales that scatter powdered light
or whispering skin, stretched on hollow bone
or latticed nets of film and vein.

Do not give me the deadness of feathers
their stifling thickness
their barbed and zipped complexity
their pigeon clatter, their blurry beat.

Do not give me wings at all
for surely I shall be beyond physics:
beyond pressure, air, bleak matter,
beyond the grey monotony of weight.

Just take me somewhere high
watch me defy the hills.

Notes

Linden Tree

In Germanic mythology the linden tree is a symbol of truth, and judicial sessions were often held under a linden tree. Herodotus talks of the Scythians using linden bark for divining.

Matryoshka

The Russian Matryoshka (nesting) dolls are traditionally crafted from the wood of the linden tree.

Golem

The golem was a figure in Jewish mythology. Golems could be created from clay, and animated either by writing the word *Emet* (תמא, "truth" in Hebrew) on their foreheads, or by placing a piece of paper inscribed with incantations in their mouths. Golems would obey instructions very literally, were extremely strong, but unable to speak.

Hoof

The horse's hoof is actually the tip of its middle digit, a result of progressive evolution whereby the other digits were lost or became vestigial. Przewalski's Horse, the only remaining truly wild horse in the world, is critically endangered. There are less than three hundred left in the wild.

Apotheosis

Parents of a severely disabled girl in the US revealed that they are keeping her child-sized in order to give her a better life… Her parents call her 'Pillow Angel'.